Leading Yourself

A Guide to Increasing Self-Awareness, Self-Alertness, and Self-Leadership.

ZEBULAN HUNDLEY, PH.D.

Copyright © 2020 by Zebulan D. Hundley

All rights reserved.

This book or any portion thereof may not be reproduced or used in any manner whatsoever without the express written permission of the publisher except for the use of brief quotations in a book review.

Printed in the United States of America

First Printing, 2020

ISBN: 9798678364890

Imprint: Independently Published

Instagram **@zeb.hundley**

www.zebulanhundley.com

iv..Leading Yourself

Dedication

This work is dedicated to my wife and children, without whom this journey would not have been possible.

I may not be able to give you the world, but I hope this opens up new worlds to all of you.

I love you.

Special Thanks

This work would not have been successful without the insights, experiences, and talents from the following amazing people:

Editor: **Jennifer Hundley**

Cover Design: **Jesse Horton**

Mentor: **Paul Scanlon**

Zebulan Hundley, Ph.D. vii

Table of Contents

Writer's Note x

Section 1 1
Self-Awareness 1

  The Journey is Art, Not Science 2
  Internal Self-Awareness 15

    What is it? 15
    How do I know if I have it? 20
    How do I develop it? 31

  External Self-Awareness 45

    What is it? 45
    How do I know if I have it? 47
    How do I develop it? 49

Section 2 65
Self-Alertness 65

  What is Self-Alertness? 66

    Obstacles to Self-Alertness 68

Removing the Blinders 79
Creating the New Paradigm 84

Section 3 88
Self-Leadership 88

The Mindset of Self-Leadership 89

    A Bias Toward What's Possible 95
    A Bias Toward Action 98
    A Bias Toward Silence 102
    A Bias Toward Discipline 105

The Practice of Self-Leadership 108

    The Daily Routine 108
    The Spirit of Excellence 114
    The Quest for Knowledge 117
    The Pursuit of Wisdom 120
    Equilibrium of Mind, Body, & Spirit 123

Section 4 127
Things to Remember 127

Find Comfort in Discomfort 128

    Comfort Is Not Conducive to Creativity 128

Zebulan Hundley, Ph.D. ix

    The Loneliness of Self-Awareness 131
    A Note About Mentors & Coaches 134
    Keys to Successful Coach / Mentor Relationships 143

About the Author **148**

WRITER'S NOTE

Since the outbreak of the COVID-19 pandemic, leaders of all walks of life have had to come to terms with a harsh reality. This reality is one that was hidden in plain sight, buried by the routine of business, and skewed by accolades and achievement. It was not until the day-to-day routine was ground to a halt that this reality came out of the shadows and began to consume the thoughts of many- even those who were considered to be strong leaders and visionaries. And when it did, it was not kind.

What is this reality? Simply put, it is the reality that the identity that these individuals were walking in was a façade. It was a counterfeit. It was based off a title, industry accolade, or paycheck. And now that the routine and system that was in place to reinforce that false identity has been ripped away, many are left wondering two things: who they are, and how they can fulfill what they feel they have been put on this earth to do.

I have had key conversations with leaders at all levels very recently who have been asking many of the same questions. Things like "What do I do to become more self-aware?" and "What exactly does self-aware mean anyway?". Now that the mundane and task-oriented day has evaporated in the traditional sense, a separation is occurring between those who have been devoting themselves to a lifestyle of growth and development to help them lead themselves and others, and those who have just called themselves leaders and maintain a checklist to prove that they are "leading".

What do I mean by this? I mean that many people that carry the title of *leader* have not been actually leading, they have only been carrying out a list of tasks provided to them by someone else; and in that process they have lost sight of the most important element of leadership- leading themselves.

If this book is to fulfill its purpose, it will help to connect you with the most authentic version of yourself and it will help you to bring into alignment two different versions of you; the version that you see and the version that everybody else sees. It is when you are able to bring these two things into alignment that you are then free to explore and expand into your fullest potential. This alignment will bring a new level of clarity, energy, and fulfillment into every aspect of life.

You see, self-leadership is the hardest (yet most essential) leadership of all. It is easy for you to see areas of improvement that are needed in those that you oversee, but it is much more difficult for you to take an honest look at yourself and to recognize that you have areas that need to be improved. It is easy to say that you are aware of your flaws, but what is that awareness doing to bring about a positive shift within you? How are you responding to this awareness? The process of gaining this self-awareness and then leading yourself from the place of your authentic self will be a key differentiator between those that will thrive in this next season and those that will not.

Full disclosure- this book is not for those who feel they already have all of the answers and who know everything about themselves. This book is not for those who are looking for validation and a sense of "I'm doing everything right". This book is for those that are committed to doing the hard work of self-examination, self-exploration, and self-leadership regardless of how difficult the journey might be.

If this resonates with you, I encourage you to take your time going through this book.

There will be statements to challenge you and questions that will require time to answer. Stop to reflect where needed. Come back to it whenever needed. This journey will not be quick and painless, but it will definitely be worth it.

I am looking forward to our journey together.

Blessings,

Zeb

Section 1

Self-Awareness

The Journey is Art, Not Science

*It is nice when others see your value.
It is life changing when YOU do.*

What is the first thing that comes to mind when you hear someone mention the term "self-awareness"? If you are like a lot of people that I have had the opportunity to connect with, you are not sure what that term means. In fact, you are also likely skeptical about the entire topic and those that claim to be able to help you on that journey. You have heard that you are supposed to have it, but you have never had anyone explain to you exactly what it looks like or feels like, let alone how to achieve it.

I understand this all too well. A quick internet search will yield a variety of opinions as to what this means. I hope to help share with you what I have learned on my own journey as a means to be your tour guide, not just your travel agent.

It is important to note the difference between these two. You see, a travel agent knows all of the marketing lingo and can give you a list of popular places to visit, but a tour guide knows where to get the best mac and cheese. The personal experience that a tour guide can bring is the difference between just an expensive vacation and a very memorable one.

Honestly, prior to going through this journey myself, it seemed as though this sense of being belonged predominately to two core groups of people – the ultra-successful and the ultra-weird. And, if I am to continue being honest, those two might have intersected in my mind more than I would like to admit. Does this connect with what you might be thinking right now?

If you are like I was, you have no idea how these two completely opposite groups of individuals seem to have come into possession of this enlightened state of being. You certainly want to be a part of the former, yet somehow without turning into the latter. You are approaching this journey both skeptical and hesitant, yet for some reason you still feel drawn to grasp this state of awareness for yourself. Either that, or your boss told you that you needed to improve in this area in your latest performance review and you're looking for where to begin. Admittedly, those are completely different scenarios, but if we are candid with one another, these are two main drivers behind this journey. People change because they want to, or because they have to. Does that about sum it up?

Let me start by asking you a question. If you were asked to name someone that was the embodiment of self-awareness, who would you name? Could you come up with a name in thirty seconds or less? Does anyone even come to mind at all? Most people will not be able to name someone. If that is you, you are not alone. If you did have someone come to mind, what is it about this person (or these people) that makes you think that they are the example to follow in this area of self-awareness?

Please do not worry or feel frustrated if you have a hard time answering these questions. Trust me when I tell you again that you are not alone. In fact, you are why this book is being written! If we are to undertake a journey to become something, it would certainly be helpful if we had a resource to help us define the *something*. Am I right?

You need to understand from the beginning that self-awareness is a journey- and a marathon journey at that. Much like any journey, there are many different roads you can take to head toward your destination. If you are an INTJ-A personality like me (if you don't know what this means, google it... trust me), you prefer to take the fastest and most efficient route to get from one place to another. If this is your natural rhythm and flow, let me just tell you that you need to prepare to slow your roll and get ready to take the scenic route. There are no shortcuts in this journey.

If you are serious about becoming self-aware, you will need to be prepared to be patient with others, patient with yourself, and be willing to intentionally slow your pace so that you can learn from everything that will reveal itself to you on this journey. A surefire way to miss out on opportunities to become more self-aware is to rush past the moments that need to breathe. It might feel like it is taking a while to get to the weightier parts of this book. This is intentional. It is designed to help you begin this journey in the proper frame of mind.

All of that said, please know that there will be moments where you feel the need to put this book down to chew on something that might be hard to swallow initially. That is not a wrong response. Just ensure that you are intentional about picking this book back up. Especially if you are one that uses the term *busy* to describe much of your life, your natural state of awareness will not lead you to do the uncomfortable work of increasing your awareness of areas in which you can- **and should**- improve. As you will see in this book, your busyness is not a reflection of your level of desire to improve. Rather, it is a function and byproduct of a schedule that has conditioned you to function from a false sense of equilibrium.

Before we begin to dig into the nuts and bolts of how to increase your self-awareness, let me first offer a few statements that will help to guide you on this journey. If you view this book (and your journey) through the lens of these statements… if you allow them to be your corrective lenses, so-to-speak, then I believe you will be on your way to living a more successful and fulfilling life.

This life will be one that is filled with so much clarity that it will simultaneously propel you forward, irritate those who wish that you would have just stayed stuck in your *back then*, and will allow you to discern between the good opportunities and the great opportunities that will be crossing your path as you are on this journey.

If this sounds like something you are interested in and you are ready to begin this journey in earnest, take these to heart:

Self-awareness is an art form, not a scientific model.

Be **aware** that self-awareness is not a simple checklist that you can mark off after reading a set of books so you can label yourself as self-aware. There certainly are some milestones you can use to measure your progress, but rest assured you will never hit a point where you have reached the peak of self-awareness and can then coast. This is a life-long journey for those that want to honestly pursue it. And this life-long journey will affect you.

It will cause you to see things that you will not be able to unsee. It will cause you to be aware of things that would have been easier to have ignored. It will cause you to be uncomfortable in familiar circles and will pull you to a place where those in your current circle may not be able to follow. That decision will be completely up to them.

___You will not be able to become self-aware without the help of other key people in your life.___

Be **aware** of those that you allow to be in your circle. Not everyone that wants to be in your circle wants to also be in your corner. If this statement scares you, please know that this book will help you to know who those people in your circle need to be (and, conversely, who you need to avoid).

Also, you need to be aware that while you can do part of this work by yourself, you will ultimately need to have one or two other people in your life that you can trust completely to help you on this journey. This does not apply to those that you currently consider friends and acquaintances. This is not to say that you have to abandon your current relationships. Rather, this speaks to the need to allow a very select one or two people to speak into your life as mentors. You will discover that there is a massive difference between those that have an emotional connection to your role in their lives and those whose sole role in your life is to help you improve.

Those that are focused only on your growth will be able to give you unbiased feedback and a window into yourself that your friends and associates will not be able to. This does not mean that your friends or associates are bad people. It is just that at the end of the day, some of your existing relationships need the old version of you. Your growth does not. If your growth is the most important thing, you need to prioritize having someone in your life that can help you progress in that growth.

This journey will not be painless.

Be **aware** that introspection will be required. Introspection is not the same as being a harsh critic of yourself. It is not my goal for you to become a self-deprecating and emotional basket case. That is unbridled self-consciousness. It is my goal to make sure you begin this journey with both eyes wide open. In fact, through this honest introspection, you might finally be able to identify insecurities that have directed more than their fair share of interactions in your life.

Likely, there will be statements in this book that will be easy to read, but hard to take to heart and even harder to put into practice. Yes, those two things- reading these principles and practicing these principles- are vastly different. The difficulty of hearing these statements does not make these statements any less true, nor their application any less necessary. In my own journey, I have found that sometimes it will really hurt to be completely honest with yourself. But, for me, I have found that as ugly as the truth may be, I can deal with the ugly truth much better than I can deal with a beautiful lie.

> *An ugly truth can make me better, but a beautiful lie always ends up tasting bitter.*

Internal Self-Awareness

What is it?

In the most simple form of the definition, internal self-awareness means that you have a good grasp on your **true identity** (not one that someone else assigned you), the values that you hold most dear, your strengths, and your weaknesses. This is important, because having this honest and complete awareness allows you to develop internal correction mechanisms (think autocorrect on your cell phone). These mechanisms will allow you to process your situations and emotions in real time, so that you respond *with* emotion without acting out *from* emotion.

It is common in today's society for someone to describe an event which caused an emotional response as a "triggering event".

Self-awareness gives you the understanding that you need so that you can install the appropriate trigger guards- preventing a negligent discharge of emotion that wounds those in your proximity.

The journey to find the answers necessary to implement this internal autocorrect is such a crucial part of our human experience, yet many fail to even begin that journey- instead settling for a cookie-cutter mold that determines what their human experience should look like and feel like. To relate this to a familiar children's story, many people settle for being a wooden marionette puppet instead of making the journey to become a *real boy.*

The unfortunate reality, though, is that for those willing to settle for an easy, cookie-cutter life, life becomes anything but easy. This is the dilemma. Do you willingly dig into this journey and uncover what has long been pushed under the rug or brushed off as a personality type, OR do you continue to live as if, somehow, you are the lone exception to the reality that everyone else on the planet has to face- the real you?

Now, I do not mean to say that the real version of you is a terrible thing. Rather, I simply mean to point out two things that we so easily lose sight of. First, that you are not as good as they think you are. Second, you are not as bad as they think you are. This can be both incredible freeing and incredibly humbling depending on how much you have allowed the expectations and opinions of others to shape your view of yourself.

As you are likely aware, determining your starting point of any journey is essential to mapping out the route needed to navigate that journey. The GPS within your automobile asks for two key pieces of information before it can generate the available routes- your destination and your starting point.

The process of becoming self-aware that is laid out in this book will not only help you map out the steps to this journey, but will help you to determine which passengers need to join you and which passengers need to stay behind. Each of these two areas are equally important in your journey. A long and difficult road trip with the wrong people can seem unbearable. But with the right people, even the most arduous journey can be one that is filled with laughter and excitement.

Also, important to note is that knowing your true self is not simply about learning your faults. An imbalanced focus on your faults can quickly turn into self-consciousness. That said, having a healthy awareness of your weaknesses along with a healthy awareness of your strengths (that you might not properly recognize) might be just the thing that is getting in the way of your next raise or promotion.

Said another way, self-awareness can bring about a knowledge of toxic behaviors that you do not know that you carry, but it can also bring about a knowledge of the true value that you have to offer to those in your circle of influence. When you have a real sense of the value that you have to offer, it removes many of the fear barriers that get in the way of conversations that need to take place in order for you to progress in many areas of your life- career, relationships, finances, etc.

How do I know if I have it?

As stated earlier, self-awareness is not a destination, but a journey. It is not something like a watch you seek to have; it is something like time that you seek to become more aware of. The more self-aware you are, the more you are able to recognize your internal self-conscious tendencies, and you are able to use that knowledge as fuel to help you grow into your next level. Self-awareness is not as much something to possess as it is something to steward.

There is, however, something you can use to measure your progress in this journey. After all, a journey without a way to measure progress is a journey that most will give up on. So how exactly do you measure where you are at in your journey to become more self-aware?

As you become more aware of who you are and what you have to offer (and improve), you begin to allow your identity to determine what opportunities you pursue instead of allowing the pursuit of opportunities distort your understanding of your true identity. This is a completely new way of looking at opportunities for most people. A typical thought process might look at an opportunity to earn more money and instantly see it as the right move. After all, if you earn more it strokes the ego inside you and it validates the effort you are putting out. However, if you allow your identity to lead your decision, you realize that not every paycheck is worth the environment required to earn it.

As you bring yourself into alignment with this paradigm, you begin to be aware the things inside of you that are revealed to be the language of the *stuck people.* And once those things are revealed to you, alignment requires that you confront these things. This is where self-leadership comes into play. But there is a later section on self-leadership. Back to the language of stuck people.

What does this stuck language sound like and how do you know if you are using it? This language uses excuses like "that's just the way I am" or "I can't help it". Stuck people will use language such as "It is what it is" and "Why bother? Nothing is going to change anyway."

Those with an increasing self-awareness will use different language. Instead of saying "that's just the way I am", they will say things like "I have been this way as long as I can remember. How do I improve this area?" The difference is not in the recognizing past behaviors but choosing to reside in them. It is amazing what that small language adjustment can make.

There is one scene in a particular movie that highlights outwardly a process that self-aware people will work to develop internally. In the movie, *"The Kings Speech"*, the character, Bertie, is dealing with a speech impediment. His speech therapist asked Bertie how long he had been dealing with this speech impediment. He was full of self-defeat and said that he was born with it. Through a process of trust-based communication, it was learned that this behavior was not something inherited at birth, instead it began at the age of four or five.

Had Bertie not had given permission to someone who was willing to dig into his life and expose a wrong, but pre-existing mindset out of care for his benefit, he would have likely stayed "stuck". The process of working with someone who had his best interest in mind unlocked another level of potential for him and he was grateful for it throughout his entire life.

Now that all of that has been said, self-awareness sounds easy enough, right? Well as I mentioned in my writer's note, most people do not excel in this journey of becoming more self-aware. For many, this is because the work is simply too hard. It is inconvenient. It takes the focus off of blame and places it squarely on the shoulders of personal responsibility. Many people seem to have lost the ability to take personal responsibility and, as a result, get lost in the framework that others have placed around them. This is not as sinister or intentional as it might sound at first.

Consider the following scenario. Think about that entrepreneur that has dedicated his or her entire life savings, every waking hour, and more energy than they thought that they had to opening up their first brick-and-mortar store. That is not an altogether unique scenario historically, but think now specifically about those that launched out and opened up their business in Atlanta, Georgia in February 2020.

So much excitement, investment in branding, receiving of inventory, time spent in marketing meetings, and the hiring and training of new employees- all to have your business shut down by mandate of the local authorities in response to the COVID-19 pandemic. All that work. All that sweat. All that risk. All that debt. All that promise. In the flick of a governor's wrist and at the same instant that an executive's signature swept across the page, all of it evaporated. Instantly. What is this entrepreneur to think? Now what?

The chances are pretty high that leading up to the moment that they were able to put the *OPEN* sign in the window, they had to convince everyone around them that they were, in fact, an entrepreneur and not "just" the guy or gal that existed in the minds of friends, family, and potential investors. Make no mistake about it, everyone holds within them a version of you that you have never met. Maybe it is a role that you filled for them or a comfort level that you provided, but I guarantee it is a different version of you than you are familiar with in your own day-to-day existence. Now, put yourself into their shoes.

So here you are. Back at square one- the dreaming phase. Everything you thought you were working for is gone and there is no end in sight. In fact, as of the current date of this writing (August 27, 2020), there seems to be no end to this pandemic in sight and in many places people are quietly (and some, not so quietly) bracing for the often-discussed second wave of this virus' spread in the United States.

Do you think this person ever battles internally over their identity and whether or not they should even be pursuing this "entrepreneur thing"? I can guarantee they are struggling with this. Entrepreneurs struggle with this under ordinary circumstances and this certainly is no ordinary circumstance. It is a form of imposter syndrome- especially for those that are launching their first business. The self-doubt is real.

In another industry, what about that young minister? He or she just graduated from a school of ministry- full of optimism about the benefit that their service to God will bring to the community to which they are getting acquainted. They receive their first ministry assignment and eagerly set out to change the world. The problem? The place they were sent to carry out that mission had invested little-to-nothing in digital capabilities prior to their arrival and in their first week on the job, their gatherings were mandated to cease and desist by the local municipalities. Chanting at a protest is fine but singing in church is somehow dangerous. Seminary did not prepare them for this kind of a legal environment.

These are not hypothetical scenarios. These are very real scenarios that are playing out daily in the United States in real time as this book is being written. How are you supposed to provide spiritual care for those that you have never met? Then adding in the additional barrier of being told that you are not allowed to even congregate with in small numbers to get acquainted and administer the duties for which you have trained for? What is a minister to do without being able to bring people together to minister to?

Can you relate to either of these scenarios? Maybe during this time of worldwide pandemic, you have not been the head of a company, but maybe- for the first time- you now understand the true meaning of the word furlough. Maybe for the first time in your life you are looking forward to things that you once shunned as beneath you- unemployment, government assistance, food pantries, etc. Are you still the breadwinner you know you were supposed to be? Does this make you question your worth or what you have to offer to your family, your friends or yourself?

In each of these situations, the sense of a physical need is great. And, too often, people allow the sense of a felt need to drive the opportunities that they pursue. Please allow me to offer the following thought for consideration. While you cannot ignore the things that you need, when you allow the feeling of what you need to drive your ambitions, you make yourself a prisoner to your feelings. When you do this, you subject yourself to making rash, knee-jerk decisions that often have poor consequences down the road.

Your feelings make great servants, but they make poor masters. Living in and making decisions based on the feeling of a need restricts you to operating in a survival mode, and does not allow you to transition into a mode of living. Being alive and living are not the same thing. Too many people figure this out after it is much too late. The good news for you? If you have the strength to read this book, then it is not too late for you. Now, your goal is to develop a greater sense of self-awareness and allow that to help you transition of simply surviving, to thriving!

How do I develop it?

I am so glad you asked! Remember earlier in the book when I mentioned the need to get a journal for this journey? This is where it really helps to have one on hand. Realistically, any piece of paper will do. That said, I believe you set yourself up for success when you have a known place that you can come back to as a reference point. If you are like me, you will find it easier to locate a journal than a scrap of paper. So, whether you have a journal or scrap paper, go and grab it and a pen or pencil before you go any further.

Now that you have your journal, it is time to connect the dots to your brilliance clues. Ok, I get it. I just sounded like one of the really weird people that I mentioned earlier in the text, didn't I. Before you write me off as one of the weird people, I am asking you to trust me here. The truest version of yourself has existed long before you knew to look for it.

Often, as we *mature,* we begin to lose sight of the real us- the authentic us- in favor of the profitable us. It is normal for our process of becoming more self-aware to require someone to help us guide ourselves back to us. It sounds counterintuitive, I know. After all, you have lived with you longer than anyone else... or have you? Have you truly lived with the real version of you, or have you lived with the version of you that you were told to be? Buckle up, because you are about to find out.

Think back to your very earliest memory. What is it? Write it down in your journal. Read that memory out loud. How does thinking about this memory make you feel? Do not rush past this moment. Allow yourself, explore it. Take a few minutes to live in that memory for the sake of this exercise. Write down what you are feeling as you think about this memory. Also, write down an explanation of why it makes you feel this way.

Pause, then come back.

You will notice that there are a few of these breaks placed intentionally in this book. This is not to say that you cannot continue nor is it designed to manipulate you. These breaks are intentionally placed to help slow down your desire to hurry up and become self-aware. You might be one of the people that are uncovering something painful in your earliest memory. It is healthy to acknowledge that pain and not just rush past it. When you use this recommendation to pause, please take it seriously. That recommendation is included for a reason. Now that that is behind us, let us proceed.

In your journal (or on another sheet of paper), make a list of the first ten moments or accomplishments that come to mind that make you feel proud of yourself. These are things that you accomplished. They did not do them, you did. No one else can take them away from you. These things give you a sense of pride. What are they? Do not overthink this, just write down the first ten moments or accomplishments that you can think of that make you feel proud. (INTJ types, I am talking to you when I mention overthinking.)

It is through the completion of exercises like these that you will begin to locate your brilliance clues. Now, what do I mean when I earlier mentioned connecting the dots between these brilliance clues? There is a very high likelihood that all of these things that you are proud of have some commonality between them. These moments and accomplishments stand out to you for a reason. What common theme does your list have? Is it a theme of helping people? Maybe a theme of leadership through difficult times? Maybe a theme of accomplishing what others thought might be impossible?

Each list is going to be different from the next. The great news is that there are no wrong answers here. You were created as a unique individual with unique gifts, talents, and solutions for the problems and opportunities that the world will place at your feet. You are in the process of identifying what all of these are. Again, there are no wrong answers here.

Once your list has been completed and the theme has been discovered, it is time to do a bit more digging inside of yourself. What are the things that you do that give you energy, no matter how much energy you give to them? It is common for people to have something that they love to do... something that they can get lost in so much that they forget to eat, sleep, etc. Is that being out in nature? Writing? Composing a song? Teaching? What is it that gives you more energy the more you give yourself to the process of getting better in that area? Write it down. It is another glimpse into your brilliance clues.

Now might be a good time to

pause and come back.

For this next exercise, it is time to think about comments that others have made to you throughout your life. Right now, I do not want you to focus on the negative comments. Rather, I want you to focus on compliments that have been given to you. Write down the first ten moments or memories that come into your mind when someone complimented how well you did something- especially if they made a comment that said you made something look easy.

These are brilliance clues. And again, do not overthink this. You do not have to reach deep into the memory bank here. If the first compliments that come to mind were given to you this morning, that is no problem. The focus is on the compliments themselves, not when they were given to you. What do these compliments have in common? Now, does this list have a theme that is similar to the themes you discovered in your prior lists?

(side note: I was serious about the journal. You are not done yet.)

A key part of identifying with your true and authentic self is intentionally taking a break from your normal daily routine to devote to connecting with those things that give you life. The chances are pretty high that when you picked up this book, you were already feeling drained from life's routine and you were tired of the lack of control that you felt you had over your circumstances. All of that is poised to change. But in order to know where your true self is going, you need to know where you have been.

So, if you are still skeptical that these exercises are going to be a benefit to you, I want to encourage you to keep going. You might, however, be a part of the camp that as you began to go through the lists mentioned earlier in this section, you began to remember your real self, your why, and your sense of purpose. Regardless of which camp you find yourself a part of, I have the same question for you.

What is different between the themes that you noticed in your lists of things that give you energy, the things that others compliment you on and say that you make easy, and the day-to-day routine that you find yourself living in now?

Is there a large gap between the time you devote to the things identified in these lists and the things that you wind up doing the remainder of the time? The narrower that gap is, the more you are walking in alignment with your authentic self. The larger the gap, the more work you have to do to bring yourself back into alignment. No one can do this for you, but this book will give you tools that you will need to make this journey a successful one.

Now, it is time for one more list. In case you do not remember, in its simplest definition internal self-awareness means that you have a good grasp on your **true identity** (not one that someone else assigned you), the values that you hold most dear, your strengths, and your weaknesses.

This next exercise is where you begin to identify **your** values. I have met many people who have taken time to craft personal values statements, only for me to find out later that they used the words that they copied from a website because they sounded good- not because they were authentic.

I have found that the best way to identify your personal values can be most easily done by looking into your pet peeves- the things that irritate you to no end. What are these? How many do you have? One, five, or ten? More or less? Whatever the number, write these down in your journal.

In which key areas do these irritants offend? Respect? Honesty? Integrity? How would you describe these areas? These are your real values. Knowing this is immensely helpful in choosing the right people to have around you as well as the right opportunities to take advantage of. It helps you weed out those people and things that are going to annoy you to no end. Know these values. Embrace these values. Do not apologize for these values. Use them as part of your compass to guide you and it will lead to greater achievement and much less frustration. You can achieve a lot of things without staying true to your values, but you cannot achieve fulfillment without staying true to them.

Knowing your true self is only one part of the self-awareness equation. It is an important starting point, but it is by no means the final stop on this journey. Knowledge without application never becomes wisdom. Remember, I told you that this journey is a marathon and not a sprint. In the coming section, we will dig into a different area of self-awareness: external self-awareness. Before you do, take time to document your journey thus far.

What themes did you discover that give you a sense of pride?

What themes did you discover that give you energy?

What themes did you discover that you can claim as values?

External Self-Awareness

What is it?

Having a healthy external self-awareness means that you know how other people perceive you. When a sense of external self-awareness is sought after improperly, it can become all-consuming and can lead to destructive behavior. That said, the desire to be aware of how others see you is healthy when kept in the proper context. It is a lack of this understanding that prevents many from gaining employment or promotion in the workplace. It is a lack of understanding in this area of your life that leads to many relational issues and an overall social awkwardness.

Those with a lack of external self-awareness will likely find it difficult to enter into meaningful relationships. Those who lose sight of a healthy level of external self-awareness will also likely experience turmoil in their existing relationships- being surprised when they hear things like "you've changed" or "you don't pay attention to me like you used to". These individuals might also find themselves emotionally wounded by a supervisor who denies a raise or promotion citing a "lack of professionalism" or "not being a team player".

Those with a lack of external self-awareness will also experience much frustration if they happen to find themselves in a management role. They will often have to default to management by title rather than leading through influence. These individuals may have great ideas, but no one will seem to want to listen- and frustration that develops from that turns quickly to finger-pointing and bitterness. The good news? You CAN develop a better understanding of how others see you if you are willing to do the work.

I will assume that if you have made it this far in the book, you are. I will not have you write down as many lists in this section of the book, but you will still want to devote some space in your journal for this section as well.

How do I know if I have it?

A great way to get a current assessment of how well you understand how others perceive you is by asking yourself a simple question.

If you were to describe yourself to other people, would it make sense to them or confuse them?

If you would describe yourself as fun-loving, would others? If you would describe yourself as generous, would others? You might describe yourself as approachable, yet your team never approaches you. If you see a large difference in your description of yourself versus the description that others would give you, there is much work to be done to bring these two versions of you into alignment.

Those who lead themselves well with a healthy external awareness will find it easier to navigate day-to-day relational experiences in the office, at home, in the supermarket, etc. They may often be described as "easy to talk to" and "a great listener". They do this by paying attention to both verbal and non-verbal cues offered by those in their surroundings. They will respect the *personal bubble* of those nearby when engaging in conversation. They will recognize when they are talking too much and they will recognize when an apology is needed.

In short, they will become quite adept at reading how others are interacting with them in the moment and will be able to make adjustments in real-time, instead of having to spend time reviewing these interactions after the fact. If you find yourself struggling in these areas, there is no need to worry. You are about to receive a few keys that can help to increase your awareness in this key area if you will put them into practice.

How do I develop it?

The first step in gaining an understanding of how *people* see you is to first gain an understanding of how an *individual person* sees you. Re-read that last sentence.

Do not skip that last step.

People are a collective of individuals. One way to lose sight of how others see you is by judging how you think groups see you instead of by judging how other individual people see you. These are completely different approaches. Think about it from the scenario of a famous rock star. That rock star might interpret the crowd's interaction with their music as personal validation. There could be a rude awakening brewing if that rock star treats people like garbage. Do not mistake the celebration of a product for the celebration of a person. This is true for anyone in the public eye.

Especially if this is not an area of strength for you, you might find it more desirable to skip this first step- because it requires much vulnerability and trust.

Especially in today's society, people have become accustomed to interacting with others from a distance through the safety of social media. And frankly, it is much easier to talk to a screen with a human being on the other side of the screen than it is to talk to a human being that is in the same room with you.

But you cannot gain a sense of how other humans are seeing and interacting with you if you always include the buffer of a screen between you. The dynamics at play are very different. Gaining an increased sense of external self-awareness may require a level of courage and boldness that you are not used to exercising. In fact, even the suggestion that you might have to interact with another human in a trust relationship might be giving you anxiety in this moment. That is okay. Breathe. Remember why you started this journey. This will help you grow.

The first step to this part of the journey happens by identifying the right people to involve in this part of your journey. Not everyone will qualify to be your partner in this awareness trek. In fact, those that you are most comfortable with are likely the last people you want to involve in this area. It is not that these people cannot answer the questions I will give you to ask them, it is that they will likely be unable to answer them with complete honesty.

This is not because they have a desire to lie to you, but because they have an emotional attachment to your response. They are used to seeing you function in a certain capacity and flow in their lives. They, as people, are naturally wired to do what is needed to maintain the status quo. Again, this does not make them bad people, but it might make them the wrong people for this part of your self-exploration.

This is because their attachment to the old version of you makes it difficult to give consistently honest feedback that will help you develop into the new version of you. As such, you will need to intentionally seek out one or two (**but no more than two**) people that you can be honest with, that will be honest with you, and that want to see you succeed in this journey.

Remember, not everyone that is in your circle is in your corner. Wait to begin the next steps until you have identified these people and have asked them if they are willing to help you as you are on this journey to develop a greater sense of external self-awareness. And be careful to find someone who is already self-aware themselves. If you choose someone who is not self-aware, they will struggle with providing you with the feedback necessary to move forward in this journey. If you cannot locate anyone to fill this role for you, you might want to consider booking a mentorship session with me to help in this section of your journey.

More information can be found on my website at

www.zebulanhundley.com

Once this person (or these two people) have been identified, you will want your journal and time to set aside that is distraction free. This next set of questions will require all involved to pay attention, answer honestly, and it will require you, specifically, to write down these answers verbatim. Start by getting an assurance from all involved that whatever questions and answers comes out stays between those in the conversation only. If you cannot trust the others involved to keep strict confidence, then you do not yet have the right people in the room.

Once everyone is on the same page, you will begin to ask very specific questions that are designed to give others the opportunity to *go there* when they otherwise would not do so. Be prepared for this. You are asking people to give you honest feedback. Some of this is feedback that you will not like. You might agree with it. You might not. The value of this exercise is <u>not</u> in whether or not you **already** see what others see, but that you **begin to see what others see**.

For the purpose of brevity, I will only give a few sample questions. It will be helpful for you to look at your own context before these questions are asked to make them more specific to you. Also, make sure that you are asking questions to people that will be able to provide feedback on them.

For example, if you ask a question that is related to how you operate or speak in the workplace, it does not make sense to ask these questions to people that have never interacted with you in the workplace. Make sense? I thought so too. That said, now that you have taken the time to get your journal and think through who you have invited to engage with you in this exercise, here are a few questions that might help you form the right questions for your upcoming conversation.

When I say _____, what do you think I mean?

When I do _____, how does it make you feel?

When I make a decision like _____, what do you think my motivation is?

Am I a good listener?

Do you feel that I understand when I need to apologize?

Do you feel that I am easy to approach when a hard topic has to be discussed? Why or why not?

Now, when you are asking these questions your primary focus should be recording these answers. You might find it easier to simply do an audio recording of the conversation using a voice memo app on your cell phone, but make sure the other person in the conversation is both aware and okay with that approach before you just start recording.

As a side note, if you would not think to ask their permission before recording something like this, you definitely need to go through this exercise!

Part of the reason that you need to be in a full-on listening mode is that you need to be paying attention to not only the words that these individuals are using, but you need to be paying attention to non-verbal behaviors as well. This will help to let you know how comfortable they are being involved in this process.

To be clear, you are not analyzing their behavior to determine whether or not they are being honest, but whether or not they are comfortable having this conversation. Believe it or not, this is part of the process of learning to become more externally self-aware. If you do not have any experience reading non-verbal cues, this book will give you a few things to look out for to help you get started.

I would recommend that you get a few books or takes a course to learn more about non-verbal communication to help develop your understanding of this key piece of communication. That said, though this is not the focus of this book, I would be doing a disservice to you by not sharing a few things I have learned over the years.

When having this conversation, watch out for the following cues that suggest that the other person might be uncomfortable answering a question or being completely open and candid with you.

- Arms crossed
- Legs turned away from you
- Avoiding eye contact

- A need to constantly sip water (or other drink)
- Laughter without the presence of a joke
- Deep sigh before answering
- Explaining their answer after seeing or hearing your reaction

All of the above physical responses are non-verbal cues that the other person is nervous and that they are preparing to become more closed off in this moment. A closed off conversation will not help you improve. Your improvement only moves at the speed of trust. You must trust the other person and they must trust you. If you need an example of what this looks like, I encourage you to watch the movie "A King's Speech" that was released in 2010.

Yes, it is the same movie I mentioned earlier in this book. It is the story of a gentleman named Lionel Logue- an Australian speech therapist- and his journey to help to overcome a speech difficulty held by a member of the British Royal Family. It is based on true events, and once the Duke of York enters Lionel Logue's consultation room, you begin to see these non-verbal cues in full force.

If you begin to notice any of these behaviors, address them quickly by injecting positive interactions into the conversation. Not in a condescending or judgmental manner, but in a way that helps them to feel more comfortable. Instead of saying "I heard that sigh, just get it out", you might say "I cannot thank you enough for helping me in this area. I do not know what I do not know, and your honesty helps me more than you know. I appreciate you."

By approaching these tense moments delicately and with honor as the base motivation, you are again reassuring the other person that their input is valuable, that you have asked for this feedback as a way to improve, and that you are mature enough to handle whatever their response might be.

This will only work in your favor if you display behavior that reinforces the fact that you are indeed mature enough to not just handle their honesty, but to respect and honor it. This will be easier for some to grasp than others, but this exercise is a part of the self-awareness journey and is a part of how to lead yourself in situations like these.

I would encourage you to pause here until you have completed all exercises up until this point.

What did you learn from these exercises in Section 1 of this book?

Did you begin more self-aware or less self-aware than you previously thought?

What was the biggest surprise that came from these exercises?

Zebulan Hundley, Ph.D. 65

Section 2

Self-Alertness

What is Self-Alertness?

> *Many are curious about their imperfections.*
> *Few are willing to confront them.*

Before we go further, let me first congratulate you on completing this much of your journey so far. Frankly, many do not have the stomach to take an honest look into who they are and to rip away the façade that they put on for others and honestly assess how others see them. Now, my question is this: how much of an alignment gap were you able to identify that exists between the version of **you** that you knew at the beginning, and the version of **you that others** see?

Awareness for the sake of awareness does not do anyone much good. It is one thing for you to be aware that you come off as aggressive and cocky. It is another thing for that to inform your approach when going into a conversation of a team-based decision-making process. It is the awareness coupled with an internal warning system that can alert you to coming triggers that can set up your situations for sustained success.

I liken this to a scenario where you are approaching a dark alley in a large metropolitan area. You can be aware of the fact that this is a dangerous situation, but if you do not also develop an alertness to specifics of your situation in a way that informs your decision whether or not to walk by yourself down that dark alley, what good is your awareness? This section will explore obstacles to self-alertness that our previous lack of self-awareness has caused and will provide you with tools needed to overcome these obstacles.

Obstacles to Self-Alertness

There is a natural tendency in all of us. That tendency is one to become less aware of things the longer that we spend time around them. This desensitizes us to things that we might have otherwise seen as a warning sign or other indicator to pay attention to.

For example, you might have an incredibly comfortable couch in your living room or den. This couch may be as much a part of your family as your pet. In all likelihood, it probably even smells an awful lot like your pet if you would take the time to give it a sniff. The problem, though, lies within your ability to smell your own pet. It is not that your nose is malfunctioning, it is that your senses have been conditioned to disregard that sensory input.

What? You do not believe me? Think about it for a moment. You are around this pet every day. The scent of the animal in your home is a part of your environment. It is *normal* for your senses, so it does not stick out as odd. Rest assured, this is not true for the visitors that come into your home. This is especially true for the visitors that do not have pets in their own home. Everything about the scent of a pet is unfamiliar to their senses.

Your guests are not used to smelling Fido. They are not used to the pet hair that will be attached to them as they leave from your home and go to their next appointed place. They certainly appreciate the comfort that your couch afforded them during their stay, but they did not appreciate the unique *bouquet* that awaited them as they sat upon the most comfortable seat in your home.

You know what I am talking about. This is the bouquet that you smell when Fido gets a bath. After all, Fido licks himself and sits promptly on the comfortable couch, transferring that less-than-pleasant wet-dog smell directly into the fabric. This unfavorable impression of the smell of your couch will undoubtedly overshadow the comfort that it afforded for your guests.

Now, I am absolutely positive that this experience was not your intent when you offered your guest your most comfortable seat. And, if they are gracious guests, they may never utter a word to you about it. But the experience was still very real. Their lack of bringing it to your attention does not mean that the experience was not very real. It is much the same when we look at all aspects of our personality and the interactions that others have when they engage with it.

Surely, if spending time around our favorite couch can blind our senses to the off-putting aroma of our beloved pet, then spending time with ourselves can do the same for other off-putting elements of our personality. We might recognize some of these parts of ourselves and try to dismiss them as *just part of who I am*, but the truth is that this excuse is "weak sauce" if you'll afford me the opportunity to speak bluntly. Remember the stuck language I described earlier? Do not get stuck in the weak sauce.

Now, you might be wondering why I just brought this up- thinking that we just went through exercises that helped us to be aware of the parts of us that are less than pleasant. And if you are thinking this, you are correct! But that is not why I used this example. I want you to think back to when your now-smelly comfortable couch was new.

Was Fido welcomed on it- muddy paws and all? How frequently did you clean that couch in an attempt to maintain its new appearance (and aroma)? What happened if something was spilled on it or if the dog brought his favorite bone up onto the couch to slobber away on the cushion? Do you remember how much you vacuumed the hair off of the couch those first few months?

Now- when did all of that change? And **why** did it change? At one time, you used to be aware that things were happening to the couch that were undesirable and when you saw them happening, it moved you to action. So, what changed? Was it the dog's behavior? Was the couch no longer something to be valued in your home? Or was it much more subtle than that? Did it just happen to fade into the background without any particular reason why? Maybe its importance simply faded into your routine of busyness?

In fact, busyness is one of the main obstacles to your self-alertness. It likely has already had an effect. Here is a quick check you can do to find out. What has your journey through this book been like so far? A few will read it quickly without applying anything inside. I am not offended by this.

I recognize that some would rather read a book about getting better simply to check a box. Some will read it as intended and will see immediate results. Many though, will begin to read it, will intend to get to these exercises, and will intend to do so in a timely manner. Then life happens. Your cellphone rings. Work happens. Distractions happen. The eagerness to get better gets swept away by deadlines and expectations that others have of you and your schedule.

Sound familiar? Hopefully, not. But for most people, that is how much of life happens. If it sounds familiar, you also likely fall into a pattern or routine that you have that helps you manage all of these other expectations. Busyness leads to routine that leads to a false sense of control. If it does not all crumble around you, you must have things handled, right? Unfortunately, while locked in this false sense of control you no longer clearly see things around you. When it feels like you have everything under your control, you stop paying attention to warning signs- often until it is too late.

Ruts happen when you confuse a lot of activity with a lot of accomplishment. Ruts happen when we are content to run without measuring whether or not we are going anywhere. Ruts happen when we put our heads down and take our focus off of our destination, trusting that our energy will get us there. Can you relate?

Another major obstacle to self-alertness comes from our natural cognitive bias toward normalcy. In simple terms, this natural tendency leads to thoughts like *something this bad has never happened before, so it will not happen now*. It causes the individual to disregard the same cautionary signs that would normally prompt them toward action.

For some, this might stem from a desire to be comfortable. If their existence has never been uncomfortable, then comfort is all they know. It will often take quite the rude awakening to better inform their decision-making process. For others, it might be a fear of the unknown that causes this normalcy bias to run so strong. An unwillingness to step out into new territory can create a strong attachment to what is known- even if that is not a good thing.

It is this type of cognitive behavior that leads some to seek safety inside the confines of dysfunctional circles and patterns of behavior (ruts). I once heard the statement: *"If you think all men are dogs, you need to first ask yourself if you are carrying dog biscuits in your pockets."* This statement speaks to the lack of awareness that can be caused by blind spots that we have allowed to develop due to our desire to be around things that look and feel *normal*.

It is not that we desire the same result, but we do not desire a different process, so we wind up getting the same results. As many of us have heard for years now, if you want something you have never had, you must be willing to do something that you have never done.

Well, friend, let me assure you that the journey you have taken up is anything but normal. In fact, you will find that as you become more aware of your authentic self and how you appear to others, you will find that you quickly outgrow the old circles, routines, and mindsets to which you have become accustomed staying within.

But in order to do so, simply being aware of these blinders is not enough. The next step in your journey is to begin removing these blinders. These are the trigger guards I wrote about in earlier pages. It is in the system of putting guards into place that the knowledge of our self-awareness begins to manifest into something that matters.

Removing the Blinders

The first step to removing these blinders is recognizing that they exist in the first place. The next is to create some type of system around your blinders that will deal uniquely with that particular blind spot. For example, let us take a look at the side-view mirrors in your car or truck.

There are many different variations of these side-view mirrors on the market. Some are a single mirror while others have multiple mirrors displaying different angles on each side. Others still have LED indicators that will flash and/or cause the internal audio system to beep in the event that something enters the blind spot of the vehicle. Some are always on. Others are triggered if the turn signal is activated.

Each system is designed with a specific function in mind. The goal for each is the same (driver safety), but how each system points the driver to that goal is completely dependent upon the vehicle in which that system is integrated. That is part of why giving each vehicle a proper test-drive is so important in the purchasing process. It gives the driver an opportunity to experience the journey with the systems that are in place to ensure a proper fit.

It is much the same with your own blind spots. For some, a system might be something as simple as having a safe-word that can be used by those trusted influences that can let you know when you are approaching a line that you do not want (or should not want) to cross. For others, it might be a daily routine that includes intentional down time to create a mental margin- allowing a space for distraction-free focus and planning.

For all, it should include the regular habit of bringing trusted voices in to repeat the exercises mentioned earlier in this book. These voices can act as a trusted compass to ensure that we are staying in proper alignment with who we are.

Now it is time for you to get to work. What systems do you need to implement in order to place the right boundaries around your blind spots so that they do not catch you off guard? If you are not sure where to start, try to step through them one at a time. On the next page, you will find a list of questions to help you step through these blind spots one at a time. After your system is in place for the first blind spot, repeat for each other blind spot as they are uncovered.

Which blind spot has the greatest chance of causing you problems?

What is one simple thing you can do to be alerted to the danger before something or someone enters that area?

Who are you going to allow to be aware of these blind spots and systems so that they can do a system check from time to time?

How often are you going to approach them and ask them to do that system check?

How will you reward yourself when your system works and you are able to head off a blind spot violation before it occurs?

Creating the New Paradigm

A paradigm is the normal pattern in which things occur. Prior to awakening to your true and authentic self, you had one way of looking at and walking through your life. This was your paradigm. It was the lens through which your vision was framed. It informed your decision-making process. It helped to determine how you defined and measured your success. Now that you have done the digging and you see both yourself and your situations differently, it is time that we create the proper lens and frame through which your future vision will be channeled.

This verbiage was chosen intentionally. When our physical vision is negatively impacted- whether due to our actions, an inherited trait, or some sort of trauma- we go to the eye doctor, have an examination, and get corrective lenses if our situation requires them. The same must be done for our internal vision, purpose, and guiding principles. So, what needs to change? If you have taken your time to go through this book with intentionality and a willingness to do the work, you have the new lens. You have been able to connect with the real and authentic you. You have been able to identify your authentic values. What comes next, is choosing your frame.

Much like regular eyeglasses, the frame serves a functional purpose. You can choose a frame that is as simple or as fancy as you would like, but the function remains the same. It holds the corrective lenses into the proper position in relation to your eyes so that the vision remains clear.

What kind of frames do you want to choose? The easy answer? The ones that you will consistently wear. It does not matter if they look great if, when you wear them, they are incredibly painful and give you a headache. If your frames are not properly fitted to you, you will not wear them.

This is true with any system or structure in your life. It has to be custom fit to your unique situation. If you try to wear frames that were designed for someone else, you will discard them at the first opportunity in favor of something more *you*. So, what structure do *you* need to create in order to ensure that the new lenses you have on yourself, your life, and your purpose stay in the proper place and are not discarded at the first opportunity?

No one can answer this question for you. We may be able to offer advice, suggestions, things that we have seen work in other situations, etc., but only with your active participation can we ensure a proper fit and finish. This is where the weight of personal responsibility and the ongoing work of self-leadership comes into play.

In the next section of this book, we will dig into mentalities, strategies, and tools you can use to help craft your own custom-made frames. Successful people are successful at one thing before they are successful at any other: self-leadership. This is the foundation upon which all other success will be built.

Section 3

Self-Leadership

The Mindset of Self-Leadership

>
> *Learn to be self-disruptive without being self-destructive.*

Self-leadership is the catalyst that makes self-awareness and self-alertness matter. Self-awareness and self-alertness are states of being. Self-leadership is a state of doing. It is when being and doing collide and begin to work in harmony that amazing things begin to happen. Communicated most simply, self-leadership is the act of taking control of your own life. It is what happens when you see something that needs to change (before you are forced to change) and you take proactive, measured steps to make the change as efficiently and effectively as possible.

Not content to sit and wait for someone else to find the solutions or to present you with options, when you begin truly leading yourself, you walk in a state of readiness (alertness) that enables you to handle with relative ease the same things that would bury the average person. When you take ownership of leading yourself, you use your awareness of self in a positive and healthy manner.

A negative use of this awareness of self would be using your weaknesses as excuses as to why something cannot change. Another negative use of self-awareness would be to use the information only to protect your ego. This could manifest inside someone in a way that they would becoming very braggadocious and domineering in an attempt to deflect from their less-positive qualities.

Conversely, a positive use of this new awareness would be leading yourself to intentionally dismantle and eliminate the toxic and destructive behaviors, attitudes, mentalities, and relationships that are revealed through this new understanding of yourself, your personality, and natural tendencies.

This is not to suggest that others are less than you when you walk in this newfound confidence and security, it is just to say that the average person walks around completely unaware of their authentic selves and, therefore, completely unprepared for anything out of the ordinary to happen. This is true for times of crisis as well as times of significant blessing.

The unfortunate truth is that if the average person's dream came true; they would not be ready to take advantage of that opportunity. They have spent all of their time talking about what they *would do* instead of showing themselves what they *could do.* That creates and environment where these same people would resent the effort it took to try to play *catch up* if the chance to live their dream appeared and they would ultimately sacrifice their dream on the altar of unpreparedness.

I do not believe that this will be the case for you. If you have made it this far in the journey, I have no doubt that you will journey on to do great things. But great things will not happen simply because we wish for them to. Great things will happen because we work for them to.

This life of achieving what most others will not will require discipline, endurance, creativity, intentionality, and a focus unlike anything you may have ever experienced. It takes a lot of effort, but it rewards a lot in return. For starters, it takes a dedication to continually grow. I know growth mindset is a trending hashtag in 2020, but a growth mindset requires much more than an Instagram or Twitter account.

A legitimate mindset that is geared toward growth requires a few unique attributes that will be discussed in the coming sections. Now, as a disclaimer, these attributes are certainly not all that this mindset requires, but these are areas where I see people frequently get stuck. My goal is not to give you a checklist to follow, but to help shape a mindset for you to walk with. This mindset requires replacing the bias toward normalcy that was discussed earlier with other biased viewpoints that will help to guide you to great things.

A Bias Toward What's Possible

I am just going to say it. Most of you will not live with this bias. It will require too much of you. It is much easier for you to think of reasons why you could not or should not try something new than it is for you to embrace the possibility of what could happen if everything goes right. For those that are willing to rewire your brain to live with this bias though, the sky is no longer even the limit. It is this mindset that took humans to space.

This bias is not the same as living life as an optimist. An optimist is one that is ultimately confident that things will work together for the good. That is not a terrible philosophy, but being overly optimistic can blind you to the realities of the journey ahead. It can create its own set of blinders that lull you into a false sense of security and a lack of planning and preparation.

Rather, living with a bias toward what is possible means that you live life in a way that you would rather say *I tried* instead of *I wonder*. It is a lens that causes you to put energy into figuring out how possible something *is* before you spend energy into figuring out how impossible that same thing is. It is placing more energy into the bucket of *what will happen if things go right?* than into the bucket of *what will happen if things go wrong?*

Self-leadership requires you to lead yourself (your thoughts, actions, and patterns) through this lens. Otherwise, how do you expect your dreams to get off the ground level? If you allow fear of what could go wrong to consume the first portion of your brainstorming session, you have made the predetermined commitment to discourage yourself rather than encourage yourself.

Why give yourself a higher mountain to climb than is already needed? Trust me, the work of fulfilling your dreams is difficult enough already without adding in extra doses of self-doubt, excuses, and discouragement. There will be enough other people trying to do that for you. Do the rare thing and encourage yourself. After all, what is the worst that could happen? You learn another way not to do something?

A Bias Toward Action

Too many people are content to plan how they will plan to plan on achieving their dreams. Now, I am all for planning. But by the time you get through with all of these planning steps, you are out of time to act. When that happens, you are left only with regret. Living with a bias toward action does not exclude planning, but it realizes that your best plans are only good until something happens that is not according to plan.

It reminds me of the difference between two friends. Both friends stated that they wanted to learn to swim. One friend went to the store and bought all of the right swimming gear. He studied about the mechanics of swimming and even took time to hire a swimming coach via Zoom (thanks Corona Virus) to give him pointers before he got into the water. He knew the *perfect* conditions in which he should learn to swim.

The problem? The conditions were never perfect, so he always had an excuse to not get into the water. It was not his fault. He would try it if only everything would line up just right. Conversely, his friend also wanted to learn to swim. One day, he went to the swimming pool. He saw that there was a lifeguard on duty, so he jumped into the pool fully clothed and learned to swim. He knew that if he did not figure it out within the time required to keep from drowning, that there was a system in place to make sure his stupid mistake did not turn into a fatal error. You see, one friend wanted to learn to swim. The other wanted to want to learn to swim.

When you live with a bias toward discussion instead of a bias toward action, you will talk a big game and we will make grand plans. You will inform others of what you will do *one day* after you have acquired all of the necessary things that you do not yet have. Eventually, those friends and family members that were- at one time or another- excited for your journey, are now bored with your lack of commitment and your unfulfilled promises. You are knowingly lying to yourself and you are lying to those around you. If this is you, stop it. Enough is enough.

As the common saying goes, talk is cheap. When you determine to live with a bias toward action, you begin to both speak and move in a spirit of excellence. This simply means doing the best you can with the best that you have. No excuses. Only execution. This does not ensure perfection, but it ensures progress. And progress, no matter how slow, is progress.

If you have not yet seen the movie, *The Boy Who Harnessed the Wind,* you need to watch it soon. It is a great example of exactly this type of thought process that the main character has taken hold of. If you find that you are one that tends to live with a bias toward discussion and you want to change this about yourself, watch this movie. Then tell yourself out loud why you cannot accomplish your task. You will hear the absurdity for yourself and it will motivate you to find a way. Guaranteed.

A Bias Toward Silence

When all is said and done would you have said more than you have done? For many people, that answer is a resounding *yes*. Much like those that are living with a bias toward discussion, these people tend to tell everyone else what their plans are, and then they get bored listening to their own voice and seem to forget about the idea. Or sometimes they deal with a much more difficult problem.

They share a great idea that is still in its most-vulnerable state (infancy) with those that do not have the capacity to understand. When this happens, those with a lack of vision seem to turn the volume up to compensate. They being to tell you why it is a crazy idea, how bad of an idea it is, and they will suddenly become master entrepreneurs in an attempt to dissect your dream before it ever has a chance to be birthed.

Learn who these people are. If they are already in your circle, change your circle. At a minimum, remove those toxic elements from your circle. But there is another way to distance yourself from their influence. Stop talking. Sometimes it really is that simple.

When you live with a bias toward silence, this is not to say that you have taken a vow of silence as some monks do. Rather, it is to live with a bias of working first and talking later. This protects your ideas in their most vulnerable state of infancy and allows your ideas to grow legs and gain strength before coming into contact with the proverbial schoolyard bullies. Walking with a bias toward silence can be difficult- especially when a new idea has completely captivated you and you want to share it with the world.

This excitement for your idea is a good thing! It is going to be needed to fuel you for your journey. But take care to share this excitement and idea with only those that are mature enough to treat it with the care it deserves. As you have already learned, not everyone that wants to be in your circle is in your corner. Some see your potential and want to ride your coattails to success because of what might be in it for THEM, not you.

If your idea is big enough to change the world, don't waste it on people who aren't big enough to change their own laundry.

A Bias Toward Discipline

Self-leadership requires an unusual commitment to discipline. When I use the term discipline, I mean maintaining a commitment to predetermining how you will respond in a variety of situations. I mean the intentional implementation of systems and structures around your life that will help you run your life and not be overrun by it. I mean a premeditated plan of action. I do **not** mean a system of punishment used to beat yourself up when something fails to go according to plan. That is not discipline, that is a useless expression of self-defeating anger and disappointment.

If self-awareness is the highway upon which you will take yourself to your next level, then discipline is the vehicle you will choose to drive on that highway. It is the set of systems and structures that allow you to set your own temperature (atmosphere), music (motivation), navigate unexpected obstacles (power steering and ABS), and redirect your GPS in the event you find yourself veering off course.

Living with a bias toward discipline does not mean that you cannot enjoy spontaneity or unplanned vacations. It simply means that you intentionally create enough margin in your life to do these spontaneous things without everything else in life coming to a screeching halt. It means holding yourself to a higher standard than others hold you to. It means recognizing your impulsive tendencies and designing a system in place to keep those in check. It means you practice hitting targets that others cannot even see. It means learning to play a sport that many others cannot even describe.

This also means that if you choose to live with a bias toward discipline, you'll be often misunderstood. You see, the average person understands procrastination. The average person understands giving up. It is part of their stuck language. Success- not failure- challenges them. Failure is familiar. Success is unfamiliar. A person with a bias toward discipline understands this difference exists. They get it- even if they might not love it. They own it. And they do not apologize for it.

The Practice of Self-Leadership

The Daily Routine

Priority Management

Perhaps the best place to begin implementing a systemic and structural change to help reinforce the real and authentic you is at the beginning. Let us get back to the basics for the moment. What does your daily schedule look like? How do you begin your day? Or does your day begin before you do?

It is easy to slip into that pattern when you allow everyone except you to put expectations on your plate for the day. When this happens, you will find that you will spend so much energy trying to *catch up* that you no longer have any energy to pursue the things that you really would like to do. When life happens this way, you will begin to feel drained, and not fulfilled.

Does this describe you? If so, how does it feel to allow everyone else to run your life? Think about that question again. How does it feel to **ALLOW** everyone else to run your life? Do you love the fact that you have handed control of your happiness to the whims of everyone and everything else? No? I did not think you would. Are you ready to take the reins of your life back into your own hands?

If you are, that begins by setting an intentional plan in place for your day- and then actually sticking to that plan. It will likely feel unnatural at first, but this is where the bias toward discipline will help you. Remember, you are committing to this. Do you still have that journal available? If so, you will want to pull it out and get ready to write in it.

Now, once you write this in your journal, it will be up to you to follow through with this. I cannot want this for you more than you want it for yourself. Unless you book a group of mentoring sessions with me, I will not be there to hold you accountable. It will not work if you are not doing this for yourself. Now, hopefully you have that journal ready and you are ready to begin.

Begin by writing down the three things in life that are most important to you. This could be related to family, spiritual matters, work, fitness, a new personal goal, or any number of other things. These three things will be different for each person. Make these three things specific. If they are too general, it will be easy to give yourself credit for a job well done when the job has been anything but done.

By writing out the three things that are most important to you, what you are doing is beginning the process of shifting your mindset from a time-management mindset to a priority-management mindset. If you wrote down five things, trim that list down to three.

This is a process you must go through to determine what you must win at- even if that means you lose at everything else. Once you have identified these three things, it is time to prioritize your schedule around them.

At the start, it may be an easier adjustment to look at a one-week timeframe- though the goal will eventually be to do this at the daily level. Start by looking at your upcoming week with a blank slate. Where do these three things need to be placed in order to be the most effective in your schedule? Place them in the proper place before you consider adding anything else.

This is priority management. Some people are morning people. Others are night owls. Each of us has a certain time of the day- maybe even a time of the week- that we find ourselves most productive. It is important to identify what time you have the most productive energy to devote to your priorities. As you begin to focus your best energy around the things that you need to be the best at, you will notice an exponential growth in these areas. Over time, you will be able to move this priority management from a weekly schedule to a daily schedule.

The key to either the daily or weekly approach is to do this BEFORE that day or week arrives. If you wait until Monday to prioritize your Monday through Friday schedule, you will already be battling the expectations that others have for your week. Get out front and lead yourself. A trigger guard against procrastination is to predetermine how you will spend your time. This way you do not leave your success to be dependent upon how you feel in the moment. Plan your week one week ahead of time. This allows you to filter the requests of others around the priorities that you have already established within yourself.

While I am not a fan of someone else planning your schedule, I would highly suggest you take my advice to intentionally schedule time for you to rest and recoup. This does not necessarily mean sleep, but it could. Rather, in this context, prioritizing rest means creating intentional space in your life for you to refresh and refuel. Your longevity in success depends on having the energy to stick around.

If you are like many others, you might find that late nights bleed into early mornings more often than they do not. Take it from someone who has tried this for years on end. This is not something that is sustainable for the long-term, unless you are determined to become an autopilot-driven workaholic machine instead of a consistently creative and inspiring force that is destined to alter the fabric of your space in the universe. You can be alive and be stuck in that restless cycle; being alive and living are two very different things.

The Spirit of Excellence

One unifying characteristic of those who are great at self-leadership is that they walk with a spirit of excellence. This does not mean that they are perfect in what they do, it simply means that their mindset and behaviors align to a specific guiding principle: *They do the best that they can with whatever they have.* It does not take the best equipment in order to be the best that you can be with the equipment that is already within your reach.

Those who are poor at self-leadership will use the lack of resources as an excuse as to why they cannot or why they should not excel in an area of life. Stated another way, great self-leaders do not focus their energy on talking about what they would do with what they do not have. They are too busy producing something with what they already have.

Another trait of those that walk with a spirit of excellence is that their excellence is not an occasional thing. Their excellence is consistent throughout every area of their life. They do not have perfect hair, and at the same time, have two-month old McDonald's bags in the back seat of their car. They do not excel only when the boss is around. Again, this does not speak to their perfection. It speaks to their consistency. Masks and façades are inconsistent, excellence is consistent.

Consistency is not accidental. It will not happen just because you want it to. It will happen when you work for it to. A common trait among all great self-leaders is their intentional consistency in the right areas. They are consistent in their decision-making processes, in the quality of the work that they produce, and in how they respond during times of crisis. Great self-leaders walk with the weight of understanding that their actions affect more than just themselves and they are determined for the wake that they leave to be a positive one.

Self-leadership gut check: In what areas of your life does your consistent excellence need to be improved?

The Quest for Knowledge

Great self-leaders understand the value of continually learning. They have an insatiable desire to gain more knowledge and understanding- and not just in areas that would be obviously connected to their career. They will actively seek out opportunities to either enhance an existing skillset or to learn a new skillset.

As a result of being fueled by a desire to dig deeper and to better understand all of the dynamics at play, they tend to push back against *"because I said so"* explanations. When was the last time you actively sought out an opportunity to learn something just for the sake of gaining new knowledge or insight?

This has been stated many ways over the years. Maybe you have heard some of these expressions? "Leaders are readers" is a popular expression of this thought. "Leaders are learners" is another. One of my favorites is

"It is not what you know that matters, but what you can learn after you know it all that does." Regardless of how it is stated, the sentiment remains the same.

Growth requires an increasing capacity to learn and understand to be coupled with the ability to navigate new challenges. This does not happen without purposefully exposing yourself to new ideas, techniques, thought processes, and opinions. Now, I certainly encourage you to be picky when deciding what new source to use as your input mechanism. That should be a given at this point in this book. But do not hold such a high view of yourself that you are unwilling to learn from someone who has yet to have your own exact experience or predisposition to a specific ideology.

Failure to explore other viewpoints only creates a feedback loop that reinforces, instead of exposing, your blinders. If self-awareness is the goal, then reinforcing your blinders should not be.

Where is it that you have created a feedback loop that is reinforcing a blind spot? Who do you know that you can intentionally connect with to help expand your information flow to help you become more aware of your existing blind spots?

The Pursuit of Wisdom

If knowledge is power, then wisdom is the learning appropriate use of that power. It is the difference between being aware and alert. It is the difference between knowing what to say and knowing whether you should say it. As a leader of other people, it is the understanding that even though you might have the authority that allows you to gain entry into certain rooms, that doing so may be a detriment to your ability to influence those within these rooms. As a leader of yourself, it is the ability for you to put into practice the lessons that some of us learned as children when watching *Jurassic Park*- just because you can, does not mean that you should.

Wisdom is not something that is free. It is quite the opposite. Wisdom costs dearly and wisdom is not gained quickly. Wisdom is more than a hashtag. Wisdom is acquired through the investment of your personal fossil fuels- time and attention. I refer to these as your personal fossil fuels because they are not renewable resources. Luckily for you, you do not have to learn all of the lessons of wisdom by stumbling over things yourself. Wisdom can be learned from the experiences of others.

But in order for this to happen, you must remove your ego and the natural desire to position yourself as the smartest person in the room. It requires you to intentionally position yourself as a student in front of a teacher who will be able to illuminate things about you and your situation that your own personal experience has not yet revealed to you. This is the value of seeking a personal mentor. This will be discussed more in depth in later sections of this book, but it is worth mentioning here as well.

One note about finding a mentor. Do not look for someone that is free. Remember, wisdom did not come to them for free. You should not expect it to come to you for free, either. If you want to use their experience to keep yourself from the pain of the lesson, at least be prepared to compensate them for it in one form or another.

Equilibrium of Mind, Body, & Spirit

Those desiring to be great self-leaders understand the importance of balance between these different facets of their lives. If you are wanting to increase the efficacy of your self-leadership, you will need to do the same. This means staying keenly aware of these three main components of your overall health(your mind, your body, and your spirit), and having systems in place to alert you that danger is headed your way before it shows up at your front door.

It is very easy to lose equilibrium between these different parts of self. This can happen when you spend an inordinate amount of time improving your physical fitness at the expense of the rest that is required for your spirit to be in balance. It can also happen when you forsake taking care of your physical self while submerging yourself in a quest to learn a new skill. Similarly, this can happen when you spend the bulk of your time living in a hyper-spiritualized state that causes you to lose touch with the physical realm that your feet are walking on.

Please, hear me. I am not against physical fitness, a quest for knowledge, or being deeply rooted in spiritual things, but I have met many people in my journey who devoted themselves so wholly to these different areas of life that they lost touch with the remaining two. This harkens back to the thoughts at the beginning of this book where activities that we are involved in become all-consuming and instead of enhancing our identity, these activities take over our identity.

Remember, you can be focused on physical fitness and still be in control of your expression of that focus. The same is true for activities designed to strengthen both your mind and your spirit. When the activities become the most important thing, the purpose behind those activities fades into the background and we can actually cause more damage to ourselves that would have been caused had we not started down these paths to begin with.

So, how do you maintain the proper focus so you do not lose your equilibrium? It begins with priority management. As was previously discussed in this section, it takes intentional time to purposefully schedule these into your week so as not to get lost or forgotten in the middle of the busyness that life will try to bring your way. My suggestion is to make all three of these areas part of your daily priorities and not just weekly priorities. These parts of YOU are such a crucial part of the fulfillment of your purpose that to ignore them for even a day can begin a downward spiral into harmful patterns of behavior.

Another key to maintaining your equilibrium is by learning to effectively use a powerful tool that you have inside of you. For some of you, it might be buried deep within. Some might not even realize that it is a tool that is available to you. But this tool is incredibly powerful. It helps you to establish and protect boundaries around the things that matter most to you. It is an expression of personal freedom and it is a tool you can use over and over without wearing it out.

What is this tool? It is learning to embrace and wield with strategic expertise the word "no". It holds more power than you might think, as long as you are willing to stick by it when you use it. Use it wisely, my friends.

Section 4

Things to Remember

Find Comfort in Discomfort

Comfort Is Not Conducive to Creativity

It has long been said that necessity is the mother of invention. It is tough to feel the push of necessity if you have created systems around your life with your comfort as your highest priority. Now, I am not advocating intentionally inflicting harm on yourself, but it is important that we recognize that if you have conditioned yourself to always be comfortable, any discomfort will feel harmful. Feeling harmful and being harmful are not always the same thing.

This is the value of bringing a coach or mentor into your life as a part of your journey to self-awareness. If you have any experience with coaches or mentors, you understand that though they can be friendly, their role is not to be your friend, but to help you get better. They are also there to help you improve in a manner that will help to keep you safe and free from injury as much as possible.

They will correct poor form and poor attitudes. A good coach or mentor will not just correct you when you do something wrong though, they will teach you the proper ways to move in order to prevent injury before learning a new routine. They will also help to celebrate you as you make progress. One of the greatest benefits that a coach or mentor can have on your journey is that they are there to root for you, to believe in you, and to help you succeed.

To be clear, that relationship will not always prioritize your comfort, but you have already determined to do the hard work necessary to grow. You just might need to remind yourself of that from time to time.

The Loneliness of Self-Awareness

I will not sugar-coat this. This journey is not for those that have a deeply ingrained need to be validated by lots of other people. In complete honesty, if you commit yourself to growing in self-awareness, self-alertness, and self-leadership, you will spend much of your journey devoid of validation from others. After all, you cannot build a palace if you need to stop construction for constant validation from the village.

If you invest in opportunities to connect to the right tribe, your experience does not have to play out in a way that you feel like a secluded hermit. There are many great people that are on this same journey and, frankly, they are some of the happiest and most authentic people I have ever met in my life. But until you find a tribe of like-minded individuals, you will often see a pattern develop where you will outgrow those who have been around you the longest. These individuals are comfortable with the old version of you. They need to be reintroduced to the new version of you- the authentic, non-mask wearing you.

When this introduction occurs, you might not understand their difficulty in processing and embracing the new version of you. After all, when you speak to them you will realize that not much has changed with or in them. They will have a much different experience when they see your new level of commitment to being the authentic version of you. It might intimidate them. This does not mean that they are bad people.

They just might not like what they see because what they see will highlight their need for growth after seeing how far along you have come. They might not see themselves as able to keep up with your new pace and trajectory. That might be hard for them to process. Give graceful opportunities for these people to acclimate to the new you, but not at the expense of losing yourself again. You cannot... you will not... ever be the same. And that is okay!

Ultimately, some will decide that they have no interest in connecting with the correct version of you. If they cannot have the old version of you, then they are prepared to walk away and will be glad to use that as leverage. Take a breath and let them walk. It might hurt for a moment, but it will ultimately be for your good.

A Note About Mentors & Coaches

Hopefully, by this point, you have already come to understand the value of having true coaches and mentors in your life. Done properly, these coaches and mentors can provide the wisdom, insight, and honest feedback you will need to continue to grow and level up in every aspect of your life. However, in the current era of the always-available Instagram guru, I feel it important to share a few insights I have learned in my own journey that might help to save you headache, heartache, and an awful lot of money.

First, please know that coaching and mentoring requires more than a hashtag or a trending meme. Unfortunately, I have lately seen advertisements on social media where I can simply pay twenty dollars and voila, I will be then certified as a life coach or other similar guide for you to trust. No experience is required other than the ability to enter a credit card number into an online form. Please do your homework before determining whether a particular individual will be the right fit as a coach or a mentor in your life. And keep in mind that you might need a few different coaches or mentors for several different aspects of your life.

For example, you would not want someone who has never been married to coach you or mentor you through issues in your marriage. They could play the role of a travel agent, but you would need a tour guide. You would need someone who walks with the weight that life experience brings. Otherwise, your mentor or coach is simply relaying information that they received from a book or online resource. You are certainly capable of doing that for yourself.

Similarly, you might have found an individual that knows how to coach you through the process of having hard conversations at work, but that knows nothing about how to properly steward his or her own finances. You certainly do not want them to play the role of your financial advisor.

All of this might seem self-explanatory; however, I see so many well-written advertisements designed to exploit individuals that are genuinely looking for help in a key area, that I felt it would be beneficial to point this out. Certainly not all coaches and mentors that you will find on Instagram are bad. I am on that platform and I certainly do not seek to take advantage of anyone. I truly seek to find those that are a good fit for all involved. So, what exactly should you look for when trying to identify a potential coach or mentor?

This surely will not be an exhaustive list, but these are key areas that you should be looking for.

Are they:

- Available?
- Approachable?
- Experienced?
- Verifiable?
- Authentic?
- Working with your best interest in mind?

Do not underestimate the importance of their availability. To be sure, the coach or mentor in your life will not be at your beck and call. They will establish boundaries of acceptable communication methods and timeframes. This is part of the process of establishing a relationship based on mutual respect and value.

That said, if you are only able to have connection with them under very specific circumstances and timeframes, you need to ensure that these circumstances and timeframes will work for you- not just them. Part of finding the right fit will include finding the right schedule.

Approachability is a foundational element to this relationship. After all, a coach or mentor is someone who enters into a mutually respectful relationship with you. If you are entertaining the prospect of working with someone who seems to lead each conversation with ego, run away as fast as you can. The authenticity required in a successful coaching or mentoring relationship is one that requires both parties to be able to be wrong and positioned such that they can learn from each other. Anything less is a counterfeit.

Do you remember the tour guide versus travel agent example that was used a few pages ago? The importance of getting this right cannot be overstated. Clearly, no one is perfect. You will not find a coach or mentor that is without a blemish on their personality or record, however if you are looking for someone to coach you on how to build a car, you better make sure that they have indeed built a car at some point in their journey. They get extra points if that car actually worked.

Do not fall for fancy gimmicks that are based on unsubstantiated claims of someone's greatness. There is a reason that word-of-mouth is the lifeline of this profession. This leads into the verifiability of the claims made by some of these internet gurus posing as coaches and mentors. Have they produced fruit that you can inspect? Can you talk to anyone who will vouch for the efficacy of their services?

Now, the nature of the coaching and mentoring profession means that we do not disclose the personal details of those with whom we are working. I understand that discretion is key. I might not disclose the names of individuals that I have worked with personally, but I have zero problems publicly attaching my name to the work that I have done within organizations in which I have held a position of trust.

If you want to verify my work, ask around. It will not take long for you to find out the personal impact that I have made on the lives of those that I have served. This is not stated out of ego, but out of verifiable confidence. Make sure that the coach or mentor that you are considering is also willing to put their confident stamp behind an organization that they have helped. It is part of what keeps us authentic. It also helps you to look at the fruit of our work and to determine whether or not our fruit belongs in your pantry.

This is not the last item to consider, but it is the last that I will cover for the sake of brevity: make sure that the coach or mentor is working with your best interest in mind. If their approach tries to fit you inside one of three pre-made packages instead of crafting an approach based on your specific need, chances are you have a travel agent and not a tour guide. Tour guides have the life experience necessary to adjust their recommendations based on your situation. They might prefer Italian cuisine, but if they find out that you favor BBQ, they will point you in the direction of something that will help you to achieve your goals- not theirs.

Keys to Successful Coach / Mentor Relationships

Once you have identified the right coach and/or mentor to help you navigate to your next level, there are a few things that you can (and should) do as the one looking to be coached or mentored to ensure that you have a successful relationship.

First, you need to understand that this is YOUR journey. YOU are desiring to improve. Therefore, the weight of ownership falls to YOU to seek out and pursue the coach or mentor for opportunities to improve. The weight of ownership falls to YOU to follow through with commitments that you have made. This includes any homework that you might have been given.

Please understand that the coach or mentor cannot want you to grow more than you want it for yourself. If you are not committed to doing what is necessary to grow and improve, it is better for you to not get started in a coaching or mentoring relationship. If you do, you risk wasting one of the greatest opportunities in your life.

I can think of more than one occasion where an individual was in conversation with me and after having their eyes opened to a blind spot in their lives, they would make statements like "Dr. Zeb, I HAVE to get an appointment with you. This hallway conversation was well worth the couple hundred dollars needed for a regular one-on-one session. I will reach out to you today to lock that appointment in." Predictably, I heard nothing from them.

Here is one key difference between a legitimate coach or mentor and a greedy salesperson. A salesperson will keep pursuing you until they have your money. Then, after they have your money, they will not care whether or not you take advantage of their services. I cannot operate that way. Frankly, your money is not worth the hassle of your company if you are not willing to follow through with the commitments that you have made. Every legitimate coach and mentor I know that has a track record of success feels the same way.

This is not to say that I am the greatest gift that your life will ever receive. However, I do know several other coaches and mentors that have shared similar experiences and frustrations. It does not take long for these coaches and mentors to refuse your appointment if you are someone who does not follow through with what you say you will do. If you want to waste the opportunity in front of you to grow, you can very easily do that. Just treat the opportunity to meet with your coach or mentor as casual and ordinary.

This journey is not something that can be treated as a hobby. Show up early, follow through, be prepared, and place the proper value on the opportunity. If you do that, I am sure you will have an enjoyable experience. I do know that if you approach your relationship this way, your coach and/or mentor will greatly appreciate the effort that you are putting in and will give you their all. This will only work out to your benefit.

Before we end our journey in this book together, I would be missing an amazing opportunity to see you win if I did not let you know that each year, I do take on a limited number of mentees and coaching opportunities designed with your success and growth in mind. If you think that we might be a good fit for one another and are interested in finding out more information about the coaching and mentoring opportunities, stop by my website at **www.zebulanhundley.com** for details.

Pro tip: It will be beneficial to you if you mention that you have already read this book.

About the Author

Zebulan D. Hundley, Ph.D.

Zebulan Hundley, Ph.D.

Zebulan Hundley (Zeb, Dr. Z, et. al.) has been formally leading people for approximately 22 years as of the date of this writing. It sounds crazy to say that, because he does not feel that old, but between the US Army, Corporate America, and leading in Church environments he has had a good bit of experience at it. Based on that experience, Zeb has also authored another book that you might enjoy:

Learning the Art of Effective Leadership

Zeb completed his Ph.D. in Church Leadership in 2017 and has been putting that knowledge and experience to use in his current position as Executive Pastor (XP) at Hope Church in Warner Robins, GA. In addition to his role as XP at Hope Church, He is also the President of Ascentient Group - a business consulting and training firm located in Middle Georgia, USA.

He also enjoys doing commercials, training videos, and audiobook voice over work- putting his voice to work in his spare time. Hey, everyone needs a break from their normal routine from time to time, right?

Zeb has had the privilege of working with some pretty great people over the years and he considers himself blessed to be able to connect with like-minded people and help to make this world a better place. Might you be one of those people? If so, connect with Zeb on Instagram **@zeb.hundley** . He would love to connect and change the world with you!

If you are interested in connecting with Zeb for coaching or mentoring opportunities, you can book an appointment directly on his website **www.zebulanhundley.com** or send an email to **info@zebulanhundley.com** for more details.